C IS FOR CIVIL RIGHTS

THE AFRICAN-AMERICAN CIVIL RIGHTS MOVEMENT

Children's History Books

BABY PROFESSOR
EDUCATION KIDS

Speedy Publishing LLC
40 E. Main St. #1156
Newark, DE 19711
www.speedypublishing.com

In this book, we're going to talk about the African-American Civil Rights Movement. So, let's get right to it!

When people mention the *"Civil Rights Movement,"* they usually mean the protests of the 1950s and 1960s that ended segregation in the United States. They think of the courage of people like the Little Rock Nine, Rosa Parks, and the great civil rights leader and Nobel Peace Prize winner, Martin Luther King, Jr.

Lyndon B. Johnson signs the Civil Rights Act of 1964.

However, the seeds of the Civil Rights Movement had started over one hundred years before their time. The fight for equality among races had started during the years prior to the Civil War.

African American slave family representing five generations all born on the plantation of J. J. Smith, Beaufort, South Carolina.

When the United States first formed, beginning with the Declaration of Independence from Britain in 1776, slavery was an acceptable way for people to get the labor they needed on their farms and plantations. However, many people thought that enslaving other people was wrong and wanted to see it change.

Slave Ship.

The Fugitive Negro.

The states that disagreed with slavery were in the northern part of the United States. Slavery was part of the lifestyle in the southern states. Wealthy landowners used slaves to work their cotton plantations. They didn't want to give up their slaves. This disagreement was the beginning of the Civil War.

An 1882 engraving entitled, THE FUGITIVE NEGRO, shows an African American running in an urban street from a mob of white men holding clubs.

BACKGROUND LEADING UP TO THE CIVIL RIGHTS MOVEMENT

The Civil War, Union soldiers in Trenches before the Battle of Petersburg, Virginia, June 9, 1864.

Four union officers in front of tent, with two African-Americans during the Petersburg Campaign.

Prior to the Civil War in the United States, the issue of slavery was already controversial, which simply means that people were divided about their thinking and the issue was hotly debated. Many people felt that keeping slaves wasn't right morally. These people were called abolitionists. Before the war broke out, many of the states in the north had taken a stand to outlaw slavery. However, there wasn't agreement throughout the nation and war broke out between the North and the South.

During the war, President Abraham Lincoln wrote a famous document called the Emancipation Proclamation. In this executive order, written during the third year of the Civil War, Lincoln freed all the slaves in the United States by executive order. When the Civil War was over in 1865, the thirteenth amendment to the constitution made it illegal to have slaves.

Abraham Lincoln (1809-1865).

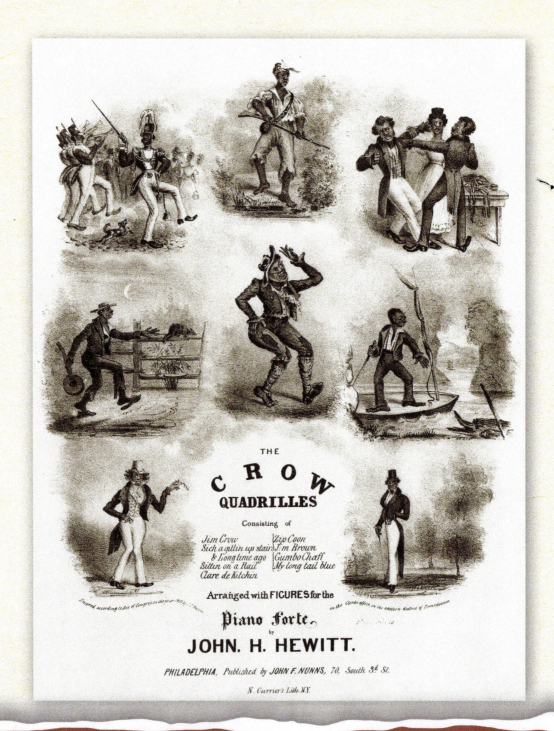

THE
CROW
QUADRILLES

Consisting of

Jim Crow   Zip Coon
Sich a gitten up stairs   I'm Brown
& Long time ago   Gumbo Chaff
Sittin on a Rail   My long tail blue
Clare de Kitchin

Arranged with FIGURES for the

Piano Forte
by
JOHN. H. HEWITT.

PHILADELPHIA, Published by JOHN F. NUNNS, 70, South 3d St.

N. Currier's Lith. N.Y.

SEGREGATION AND THE JIM CROW LAWS

Despite the fact that it was now illegal to have slaves, in the South, African-Americans weren't treated the same way as white people were treated. They were treated as if they were *"second-class citizens."* This means that they were segregated from other people and not given the same rights. States in the south put Jim Crow laws into place.

Sheet music entitled the Crow Quadrilles, I and illustrated with several caricatures of African Americans.

These laws kept African-Americans separate from Caucasians so they weren't able to sit in the same areas on buses and trains, attend the same schools, or eat at the same restaurants. They weren't allowed to use the same restrooms or drink from the same water fountains simply because of the color of their skin. There were laws in place that prevented them from expressing their right to vote as well.

Flag announcing another lynching.

EARLY PROTESTS AGAINST THE JIM CROW LAWS

African-Americans began to protest against segregation and the Jim Crow laws in the early part of the 1900s. In 1901, several prominent African-American leaders such as Ida B. Wells, who was a journalist and activist, and W.E.B Du Bois, who was the first African-American to earn a Ph.D. from Harvard University, collaborated to form the NAACP, the National Association for the Advancement of Colored People.

Sign reading 'waiting room for colored only, by order Police Dept.' Ca. 1940s or 1950s.

Another important educator and leader was Booker T. Washington. A former slave, Washington taught himself to read and write and eventually established schools so that freed slaves could get an education and improve their chances for success in society.

*James Meredith walking to class,
protected by U.S. Marshals.*

THE CIVIL RIGHTS MOVEMENT GROWS

Then, something happened that was a turning point in the Civil Rights Movement. In 1954, there was a famous court case that was brought to the Supreme Court. At that time, public schools were still segregated by race.

It was thought that even though black children and white children weren't going to the same schools that it was acceptable as long as the education the children were getting was the same. In other words, the policy was *"separate, but equal."*

Attempting to block integration at the University of Alabama, Governor of Alabama George Wallace stands at the door of Foster Auditorium while being confronted by US Deputy Attorney General Nicholas Katzenbach.

Vivian Malone Jones arrives to register for classes at the University of Alabama's Foster Auditorium.

Oliver Brown sued the city of Topeka, Kansas because he wanted his child to attend an all-white school. He argued that his child wasn't getting the best education possible because the schools weren't equal. The case made it to the Supreme Court. After studying the situation, it was found that even if educational quality was similar, the mere fact of segregation made children in the black schools feel inferior and therefore the situation was unequal.

The Supreme Court ruled that segregation was against the law and that schools must integrate so that students of all races were attending all schools. Then, in Little Rock, Arkansas, nine brave African-American students, eventually called the Little Rock Nine, took a stand as they tried to attend a high school that was all white.

Soldiers from the 101st Airborne Division escort the Little Rock Nine students into the all-white Central High School in Little Rock, Arkansas.

M

Many white people were unhappy about the situation and tried to prevent the students from entering the school with violence and ugly verbal threats.

Little Rock, 1959. Rally at state capitol. Photograph shows a group of people, one holding a Confederate flag, surrounding speakers and National Guard, protesting the admission of the "Little Rock Nine" to Central High School.

At the beginning, the governor of Arkansas tried to prevent them from entering the school saying that he wanted to avoid violence in the town.

President Dwight D. Eisenhower had to enforce the desegregation with federal troops, but the battle wasn't over yet.

Robert F. Wagner with Little Rock students.

These courageous students were able to attend the school but sadly, they were subjected to abuse by the white students. It took from 1957 until 1972 for all the schools in Little Rock to have attendance by both black and white students.

Robert F. Kennedy speaking to a Civil Rights crowd in front of the Justice Department building, June 1963.

TURNING POINTS IN THE MOVEMENT

Another courageous African-American was a woman by the name of Rosa Parks. On the first day of December in 1955, she picked a seat on the bus to rest after a hard day at work. At this time, the buses in Montgomery, Alabama had separate but equal seating. This meant that the bus driver made all the African-American passengers sit at the back of the bus.

Rosa Parks being fingerprinted by Deputy Sheriff D.H. Lackey after being arrested for boycotting public transportation.

Montgomery, AL: Rosa Parks, 43, sits in the front of a city bus.

All the seats were filled when the bus driver stopped to pick up some white passengers. The bus driver told Rosa that she and some other African-American passengers would have to give their seats to the white passengers. Rosa refused to get up and give up her seat. The bus driver threatened to have her arrested, but Rosa still didn't move. The police arrested Rosa and put her in jail.

However, her bravery didn't go unnoticed. A group of African-American leaders had a meeting. They decided that the best action they could take would be to boycott the public transit system. A young Dr. Martin Luther King was one of the leaders in this group, which was called the Montgomery Improvement Association.

Photograph of Rosa Parks with Dr. Martin Luther King jr. (ca. 1955).

March on Washington, Aug 28, 1963.

It wasn't easy for the African-American population of Montgomery to boycott the buses. They had to walk or ride in a carpool to get to work. They couldn't easily get into town to buy the things they needed. However, they knew it was important to be united in their cause. They stayed firm in their resolve for 381 days. Finally, the Supreme Court rewarded their efforts by ruling that the state laws enforcing segregation in the state of Alabama were against federal law.

MARTIN LUTHER KING, JUNIOR

Martin Luther King Jr. Memorial, Washington DC.

Photo of Dr. Martin Luther King, Jr. being arrested in Montgomery, Alabama. 1958.

During the Montgomery boycott, Dr. Martin Luther King, Jr. was arrested and a bomb was set off in his home. Dr. King, a Baptist minister with strong Christian values, believed in using nonviolent protests for social change. He was inspired by Mahatma Gandhi, the leader of the independence movement in India, who had used peaceful protests to point the way for societal changes.

Dr. King was an educated man and a masterful speaker. He knew how to inspire people with the courage needed for standing firm during nonviolent protests.

Martin Luther King, Jr.

During his short lifetime, Dr. King led many nonviolent protests, but one of the most famous is the *"March on Washington."* In 1963, Dr. King helped to organize this march, in which over a quarter of a million people participated. The goal of the march was to show their support of important legislation for the civil rights of African-Americans.

Civil Rights March on Washington, D.C. (Dr. Martin Luther King, Jr. and Mathew Ahmann in a crowd.)

The participants wanted to end all segregation in schools at all grade levels. They wanted laws that would prevent employers discriminating against job candidates based on the color of their skin. They also wanted laws to protect them against unwarranted abuse by the police force.

Martin Luther King - March on Washington.

Martin Luther King Jr. addresses a crowd from the steps of the Lincoln Memorial where he delivered his famous, "I Have a Dream," speech

It was at this march that Dr. King delivered what would end up becoming one of the most famous speeches in history. It was a speech called *"I Have a Dream,"* which he gave at the steps of the Lincoln Memorial in Washington D.C. This inspiring speech showed the world that African-Americans and others who supported the cause for equality for all races would prevail. A year after the March on Washington, the Civil Rights Act was passed, which outlaws discrimination.

The Civil Rights Movement, like other movements in the past, had converted American democracy. It functioned as an exemplary for group development comprising students, gays, lesbians, women and others.

Awesome! Now you know more about the Civil Rights Movement in the United States. You can find more History books from Baby Professor by searching the website of your favorite book retailer.

MLK Jr's I Have a Dream speech location.

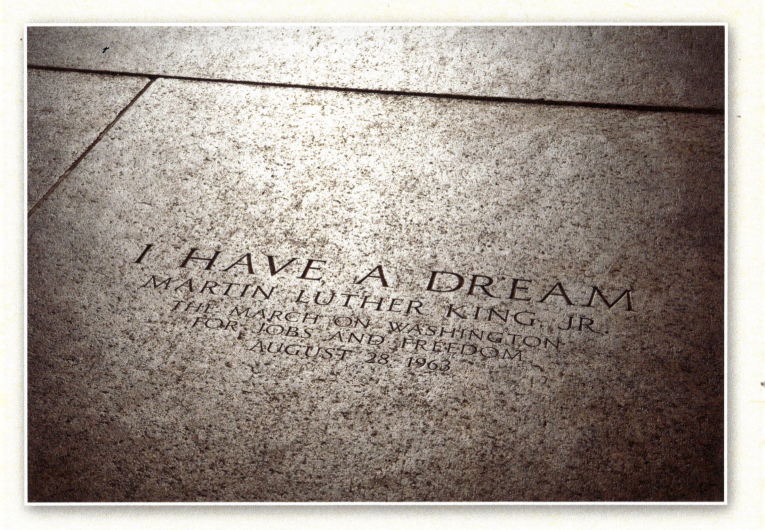

Visit

BABY PROFESSOR
EDUCATION KIDS

www.BabyProfessorBooks.com

to download Free Baby Professor eBooks
and view our catalog of new and exciting
Children's Books